TRAMS, BUSES & TROLLEYBUSES
Past and Present

No 3 KENT

MAIDSTONE: By the time this picture was taken looking in the opposite direction from Maidstone Town Hall in around 1950, your average trolleybus was a handsome-looking vehicle when seen from any angle, and here is one of 12 Sunbeams with Northern Counties bodies delivered in 1947, heading for Loose. When I arrived in Maidstone, usually by Maidstone & District route 7 from Tonbridge, I was always amused by the notion that the trolleybuses ran from Barming to Loose. Among the cars that today would grace any vintage rally are a large Wolseley saloon, so beloved of police forces all over the country, a Morris Commercial van and a wartime vintage Bedford 3-ton lorry.

The second picture, taken from ground level, shows Christmas lights in the High Street in December 1994. *KPA Goulding/author*

TRAMS, BUSES & TROLLEYBUSES

Past and Present

No 3 KENT

Michael H. C. Baker

Past & Present Publishing Ltd

First published in 2017

British Library Cataloguing in Publication Data

A catalogue record for this book is available from the British Library.

ISBN 978 1 85895 298 7

Past & Present Publishing Ltd
The Trundle
Ringstead Road
Great Addington
Kettering
Northants NN14 4BW

Tel/Fax: 01536 330588
email: sales@nostalgiacollection.com
Website: www.nostalgiacollection.com

Printed and bound in the Czech Republic

Unless otherwise credited, all pictures were taken by the author.

To John Lines MBE, a good guy

DEAL: To mark the centenary of the East Kent Road Car Company, to give it its proper title, a rally was held on 3 September 2016 in Deal, where the company can claim to have its origins. Here Daimler Fleetline RFN 953G with a Park Royal body dating from 1969 leads a modern Stagecoach East Kent Solo on a local Deal/Walmer service, with, just visible in the distance amongst the traffic, a Park Royal-bodied Dennis Lancet coach, EFN 592, of 1950.

CONTENTS

WILLESBOROUGH: Passing through the village heading for Ashford in September 2009 is a Stagecoach East Kent Dennis Trident.

BROADSTAIRS:
As mentioned in the Introduction, my first memory of a journey to Kent is by coach to Broadstairs. Here are Mum, Granny, Aunt Ada and myself on the beach in 1939. Some seven decades later I was photographing CUL 162V, a former London Transport Leyland Olympian, in the town in 2010.

Finally, on 25 August 2016 Stagecoach East Kent No 15270 (YN16 WVK) inches through the holiday traffic, with the English Channel visible at the end of the main street.

INTRODUCTION

I have lived in Kent, off and on, over the years, but my first memory of a journey to the county – and it's a very early one – is by coach to Broadstairs. This must have been in the last summer before the outbreak of the Second World War when I would have been two years old. My one memory of that visit is of watching the big cutting wheel in a butcher's shop slicing into a side of bacon. Goodness knows why that, rather than the delights of the beach, should have stuck in my memory, and how I know it was Broadstairs and that we travelled by coach I cannot explain, but it's not the sort of thing parents would have told me about later, so there it is. Many, many coach companies ran day or longer trips to the Kent coast from the London area, and some still do. We were living in Croydon, and the odds are that we travelled either in an ochre and brown John Bennetts coach, probably an early Leyland Tiger, or a predominantly grey Bourne & Balmer – later absorbed by Timpsons – Dennis Lance or AEC Regal.

Kent is a county of contrasts, more than most. Up in the far north-west corner it has been absorbed by Greater London, but nevertheless if you are an ambitious cricketer or any particularly skilled sportsperson and live in Deptford, Catford or Greenwich, to give three examples, you may well qualify to play for Kent. Further east along the banks of the Thames, where the Medway flows into the estuary at Sheerness, is an area that was once very industrial, and to a degree still is. Chatham was for long one of the principal homes of the Royal Navy, and the historic dockyard is a crowd-puller. This and the surrounding, heavily industrialised areas of Gillingham and Rainham provided much business for the Chatham & District Tramways and, from 1929, its buses. Ancient, picturesque Rochester, with its cathedral and castle in particular, is steeped in associations with Charles Dickens, as is so much of North Kent.

Indeed, Kent in general has an indisputable claim as the inspiration for that greatest of all English storytellers. Every time I cross Blackheath on a Transport for London No 54 I picture the Dover coach being stopped on its way to the Channel coast in *A Tale of Two Cities*; David Copperfield found refuge with his aunt on the Kent coast; Pip found terror on the marshes beyond Gravesend; and the members of the Pickwick Club met with adventures all over the county.

Holidaying in Kent, particularly in Broadstairs, Ramsgate and Margate, was a family tradition, extending back to Victorian times when my grandparents were young and raising their family of three boys. In one of our albums I found a couple of postcards of the little four-wheel American-built cars of 'the most picturesque tramway in Kent', to quote Baddeley and Price, running along the promenade at Margate. I was in Margate last week and perhaps surprisingly the scene is far from totally changed. There were a number of tramways in Kent, some of them very short-lived, but some survived long enough to be replaced by trolleybuses.

Inevitably it is the two great BUT companies of Maidstone & District and East Kent that one thinks of first of all, and their vehicles feature in most of our pictures, together with those of London Transport. All three have, not surprisingly, been the focus of dedicated preservationists, and we have to thank these splendid folk that the traditional liveries, once so familiar in city, town, country and seaside, live on.

Growing up in a London suburb I accepted it as a fact that red double-deck buses were almost inevitably AECs. Southdown coaches passed

the end of our road, and we had lived for a time in Bognor, so I knew that coaches and seaside buses were green Leylands. However, when holidaying in seaside Kent a year or so after the war I was somewhat taken aback to discover that AEC double-deckers, and single-deckers for that matter, could also be found beside the sea, wearing the distinctly appealing darker green and lined pale cream of Maidstone & District. Mind you, there were just as many Leylands. As for East Kent, well, like Southdown, that was also a predominantly Leyland concern, although it went in for Dennis single-deckers in a big way. The livery was a deep red, almost identical to that of Ribble I would discover later, which in its preference for the Leyland make in some ways paralleled both Southdown and East Kent. The coaches of all three big South of England companies were especially attractive, both in shape and livery. East Kent seemed to be totally committed to the Leyland make for its coaches, but Maidstone & District had a lot of AECs and, in their two-tone livery, introduced around 1947, and that magnificent encircled fleet name, they were very nearly the most handsome vehicles on the road.

Most unusually for a BUT company, Maidstone & District had a penchant for Bristols, especially double-deckers; none had ECW bodies, although some single-deck Ls with AEC engines did. After buying a fleet of PD1s and a single PD2, East Kent switched its allegiance to first Guy, then AEC double-deckers. There were some post-war Dennis Lancet half-cabs and a batch of early underfloor Lancet coaches, but for a long time after that AEC dominated the coach and single-deck bus fleets – which were in a sense one and the same thing. Maidstone & District embraced the rear-engined Atlantean era enthusiastically, but East Kent kept hold of the half-cab AEC Regent, then the Bridgemaster, which was possibly the ugliest bus of its era, and looked even worse in dull, badly weathering NBC livery.

But for all that there was always something interesting going on in Kent, and the preservationists have ensured that working examples are out and about, the modern bus and coach have much to recommend them, not least in design and comfort, which are, thank goodness, so much better than the gloomy National Bus Company days, now also a distant memory.

WESTMINSTER: Among this wonderful group of coaches outside Westminster Abbey in the early 1930s is an East Kent Tilling-Stevens. *Author's collection*

Kent buses in London

VICTORIA: East Kent JG 5422, a Leyland TS7 Tiger with a Park Royal body of 1935, has just arrived at Victoria Coach Station in June 1955. This handsome vehicle stayed with the company for 20 years.

Above: VICTORIA: A contrasting group of Maidstone & District coaches stands at Victoria in April 1955. Nearest the camera is No CO556 (DKT 14) , a Leyland TS7 Tiger of 1937 with a 1949 Harrington body, which served the company for 21 years. Beyond are two Harrington-bodied AEC Reliances of 1954.

Left: VICTORIA: No CO554 (DKT 12) is another 1937 Leyland TS7 Tiger, this time with a 1950 Harrington body. *Author's collection*

Above: VICTORIA: Maidstone & District, East Kent and Southdown all took a shine to the notion of fitting Beadle coach bodies to pre-war AEC and Leyland running units whose bodies were no longer fit for use. East Kent GFN 269 of 1952 waits to take passengers for onward flight to Paris *Author's collection*

VICTORIA: These two Maidstone & District vehicles are Harrington-bodied 37-seat Reliances of 1954.

VICTORIA: During the double-deck era at Victoria in the early 1980s, one of the massive Maidstone & District 72-seat ECW-bodied Leyland Olympians of 1983 stands on the far left. The hair styles are of the period too.

In the line-up of coaches at Victoria on 23 May 2016, a Stagecoach East Kent example is nearest the camera.

VICTORIA: Maidstone & District embraced the Leyland Atlantean with great enthusiasm, being among the very first purchasers of this revolutionary rear-engined vehicle. This is No DH570 (570 LKB), a Metro-Cammell-bodied 77-seat example delivered in 1960, pressed into long-distance service when virtually new. *Author's collection*

VICTORIA: Boarding the 10.30am National Express departure for Canterbury and the Kent coast on 23 May 2016.

VICTORIA: Vehicles awaiting their return journeys were at one time parked in the side streets all around the coach station. Taking a rest a couple of streets away from Victoria in August 1954 is No SO2 (GKR 612), one of three Bristol L5Gs delivered in December 1941 and fitted with a utility 35-seat body by Strachans. Hardly ideal for a long-distance journey from the Kent coast, it was withdrawn later that year.

VICTORIA: A very much more refined vehicle, No CO32 (JKM 432) is a Mark 1 AEC Regal of 1948 with a handsome 32-seat Beadle body, and is seen near Victoria in April 1955. However, in looks, if not in interior appointments, by the mid-1950s it was decidedly old-fashioned, and Maidstone & District disposed of it after 11 years' service.

BATTERSEA PARK: Coaches were also parked on what had once been railway land at Battersea Park on the edge of the Thames. East Kent's CFN 89 was one of a large batch of Park Royal-bodied Leyland PS1 Tigers of 1947, bought to make up for the many company coaches that went for war service and were never returned. From 1920 onwards motor coaches conveyed holidaymakers and day-trippers to the Thanet coast in considerable comfort, and another East Kent Park Royal-bodied Tiger, CFN 104, of 1948 has been preserved.

LIVERPOOL STREET: Kentish Bus Dennis Dart L126 YVK is at Liverpool Street in 1996, leading a line of buses; bringing up the rear is a Metrobus working what is probably London's most famous bus route, the 11.

STRAND: One of the most surprising consequences of Kentish Bus obtaining the contract to operate route 19 in 1992 was Routemasters appearing in central London, Strand in particular, in the attractive Kentish Bus livery.

London: old Kent roads

NEW CROSS: The extreme south-east corner of what is now Greater London used to be part of Kent. One such modern suburb is New Cross, only 4½ miles from Charing Cross, and the location of London's largest tram depot. During the last week of the trams, in July 1952, entering the depot is E3 No 1966, while leaving is HR2 No 1875. These trams had identical bodies, dating from 1930, but the HR2 was more powerful, designed for hilly routes. Just partly visible, sneaking out of the picture on the right and heading east along New Cross Road, is a post-war East Kent Leyland Tiger PS1 coach. *Author's collection*

ELEPHANT & CASTLE: In the past, as today, coaches departing from Victoria picked up passengers at several points in south-east London, and here on 23 May 2016 a number are about to board in New Kent Road, Elephant & Castle.

Right: **OLD KENT ROAD:** The flyover forming the background of this picture takes coaches bound for the Kent coast from New Kent Road onto Old Kent Road. The bus destined for its Old Kent Road terminus is newly delivered Transport for London New Routemaster No LT552, designed by Heatherwick and built in Ballymena, Northern Ireland.

CAMBERWELL: Including Camberwell is a bit of a cheat in that it was actually in Surrey. But

my excuse is that I've always thought of it as Kent since it was east of the tram and bus routes I used to get from Thornton Heath to central London. Anyhow, it is almost in Kent for if you travel north up Camberwell Road it will bring you to Elephant & Castle – turn right and you are in New Kent Road, which very shortly becomes the celebrated Old Kent Road. The first picture, dating from around 1947 and taken in Camberwell Road beside Camberwell Green, shows an E1 tram nearest the camera, then an HR2, and ahead of them at the kerb an STL on route 68. The E1 was built in 1922, although many examples still running dated back to 1907, the year the class was introduced by London County Council. The HR2, also an LCC design, dates from 1930/31, and the STL from some time in the 1930s. Scrapping of the E1s began in 1938 but getting on for half the class survived the war, none being withdrawn after 1940, but scrapping recommenced and all of them, apart from two preserved examples, had gone by the end of 1951. The HR2s lasted until the very end, in 1952, and one survives. The STL design originated in London General days, but was developed by the London Transport Passenger Board as its standard double-deck, diesel-engine bus of the 1930s. Four survive, together with one post-war more or less standard provincial example of 1946.

At the same location, but on the opposite side of the road in July 2014, is New Routemaster No LT146, seen at its destination. *Author's collection/author*

17

Left: **CAMBERWELL: E3 tram No 1908 heads through Camberwell for Grove Park, which was as near trams ever got to Bromley town centre. Behind it are a Maidstone & District AEC Regal coach and a roof-box RT** *Author's collection*

Below: **GREENWICH was certainly in Kent, and on 22 April 1951 E3 tram No 1871 is bound for Victoria, while in the background E1 No 840 is about to make a return journey to London.**

At the same location today, seemingly little has changed except that a great deal of paint and tender loving care has been applied to the buildings of largely Victorian origin. The bus is almost new Stagecoach ADL No 13083 (BL65 OYB). *Pamlin Prints/author*

GREENWICH: A Kentish Bus Dennis Dart stands ahead of a Londonlinks Volvo at Greenwich in May 1997. Londonlinks, based in Maidstone, took over most of the London-based Kentish bus routes in January 1995, but the Dart has not yet been repainted. Londonlinks merged with Maidstone & District in June 1996, and thus became part of the Cowie group and, subsequently, Arriva.

The second similar Greenwich scene features GoAhead Enviro No SE210 in April 2016. In the background is the *Cutty Sark*, the famous clipper ship of 1862, which arrived for preservation in dry dock at Greenwich in 1954, two years after the last trams had quit the town's streets.

WOOLWICH: B2 trolleybus No 95 (CGF 95) is seen in Beresford Square in the mid-1930s. The wholesale replacement by London Transport of its tram system with trolleybuses began with the Dartford and Bexleyheath routes, among others, on 10 November 1935. The B2s were shorter than the later, longer, 72-seat vehicles, and soon proved inadequate for the Woolwich area. The entrance to Woolwich Arsenal can be seen in the background.

Trams continued to run westwards from Woolwich to central London for another 17 years. In this 1948 picture *(Left)* former West Ham Corporation E1 tram No 337, dating from 1925, is seen in Beresford Square; note the market stalls on the right. The West Ham version of the E1 lasted until the very end of the first generation of London trams, Saturday 5 July 1952.

The third view shows the same location again on 22 February 1977. London has many street markets, and that in Beresford Square, in all its diversity, is one of the best known.

Finally we see Beresford Square today, and there are few places in the London suburbs where the ethnic mix is more apparent. *Author's collection (2)/Author (2)*

WOOLWICH: No RT1762 of Sidcup Garage bumps its way over the cobbles in Beresford Square in 1977. Both cobbles and the tram tracks lasted into the 1980s before the Square was gentrified and buses banished. The headgear of the passengers would not have looked out of place on a tram 25 years earlier.

WOOLWICH: The tram tracks lasted in the Square for decades after the trams had disappeared. No RT1762 (KYY 600) is negotiating them, cobbles in all, in February 1977.

WOOLWICH: Kentish Bus MCW midibus E33 NEF waits in the town centre in June 1996.

WOOLWICH: Stagecoach Enviro 400 No 19186 (LX11 BKJ) is on trolleybus replacement route 96 in the town centre on 24 May 2016.

WOOLWICH: Today route 51, which runs from Orpington station to Woolwich, terminates in the High Street, within sight of the river, where Selkent Scania No 15041 (LX09 AAU) is seen in 2014.

Right and below: **WOOLWICH:** No RT2345 is seen heading down Grand Depot Road towards Woolwich town centre in 1972.

Times change! At the same location on 24 May 2016 traffic queuing to board the Woolwich Free Ferry is stretching all the way up Grand Depot Road, while the driver of a GoAhead Enviro 200 begins to ease his way out so he can turn left and head for Woolwich town centre.

CATFORD: The rather handsome garage at Catford was built by Thomas Tilling before the First World War and in this scene, taken some time in the early 1920s, Tilling–Stevens petrol-electrics are prominent.

The garage in 2010 is seemingly unchanged in more than 80 years. The buses are Selkent Tridents, one taking a rest from working route 47. *Author's collection/author*

CATFORD: The petrol-electrics were replaced by standard AEC Regents but fitted with Thomas Tilling's own distinctive bodies. One of the later varieties, which in 1933 would be absorbed by London Transport into the STL type, stands outside Catford garage in about 1932.

One Tilling ST survives, No ST922 (JG 2098), a prize exhibit at the London Bus Museum, Brooklands. It is seen here swinging around Parliament Square on a visit to central London. *Author's collection/author*

CATFORD: This view outside the garage is looking north in 1950. The tram, No 574, is one of the 1930-vintage E1s, the final examples of a type originating from 1907 – and perpetuating such an archaic design did nothing to aid the trams' fight for existence with the AEC Regent and the Leyland Titan. On the left is AEC Regent No RT1357 working the long-established route 47 to central London, and on the right No RT530 is bound for the semi-rural delights of Selsdon. *Rev A. W. V. Mace*

CATFORD: Timpsons was a major London coach operator and worked regularly to the Kent coast. On the right is the company's garage and offices at Catford undergoing refurbishment in about 1950, with a rebuilt London Transport ME3 tram passing. Timpsons took over the Croydon firm of Bourne & Balmer in 1953, but retained that company's livery until 1960; it was in one of the firm's coaches that we employees of the *Croydon Advertiser* made our annual staff outing, to Canterbury, in 1954.

CROYDON: A most impressive line of Timpsons AEC Regal coaches is parked in North End, Croydon, in about 1935. One coach was quite sufficient for the *Advertiser* staff outing, so this was obviously something on a much grander scale.

Corgi made this rather nice 1:50 scale model of a Timpsons Duple-bodied AEC Regal 111.

BECKENHAM: No RF369 (MXX 11) inches its way through the traffic in Beckenham High Street in 1955. The RF was introduced by London Transport in 1950 and in all 700 were built, encompassing private hire and Green Line coaches, and Central and Country Area buses. In 1955 the route 227 still employed conductors, like most bus routes worked by the RFs, although eventually one-person operation would become the norm.

Metrobus Enviro 200 No 175 (YX61 ENT) has rather more room in Beckenham High Street on a May evening in 2016.

BECKENHAM JUNCTION: Trams returned to Kent in May 2000 when Croydon Tramlink reached Beckenham Junction, taking over a former railway line. In the first picture, taken in 2002, a tram is on the far left at the station, while taking centre stage is a Stagecoach Plaxton-bodied Dennis Dart.

On 24 May 2016, repainted and refurbished tram No 2533 catches the rays of the setting sun at Beckenham Junction.

BROMLEY was an ancient Kent market town that gained its charter in 1258, but by the end of the 19th century was on the cusp of becoming a London suburb. Two London Transport Country Area routes, the 410 and the 402, met red buses here. Perhaps surprisingly, the latter service still connects Bromley with Tonbridge, and indeed – more surprisingly but logically – has been extended southwards to Tunbridge Wells. No STL477 (AYV 634) takes on a full load of passengers at the Bromley terminus of the 402. By the looks of the open windows and the customers' attire it is a warm summer day. We don't know the precise date but it's likely to be either 1945 or 1946, for No STL477 has its wartime white mudguard markings, but the netting that protected the windows against bomb blast has gone. The bus is in red Central livery. None of these early STLs originally worked in the Country Area, but many were transferred there during the war, although it sometimes took several years for them to acquire a coat of green and white paint. *Author's collection*

BROMLEY: Occasionally single-deckers worked the 410, and here is one of the unique side-engine AEC Qs, No Q40 (CGJ 165), at the Bromley terminus in about 1949. Although experimental, the Q type in its various forms served London Transport well throughout the war years and beyond, and was only taken out of service when its direct successor, the underfloor-engine AEC Mark IV Regal, the RF, went into production in 1950. *Author's collection*

BROMLEY: For a time minibuses, known rather disparagingly as 'bread vans', were much in vogue, and here one of 1974 vintage is seen at work in the town centre.

BROMLEY was the last London Transport garage south of the Thames to work RTs. No RT492 (HLX 309) is seen in the town centre in April 1976, shortly before withdrawal.

BROMLEY: A Kentish Bus Lynx stops in the town centre in May 1997, having worked the 227 service from Crystal Palace and Beckenham. Meanwhile a Metrobus Dart heads westwards.

BROMLEY: A very wet day in the town in 2012.

West Kent: Westerham, Sevenoaks and Edenbridge

GODSTONE: The 410 was a particularly interesting and well-known route, as it served the Biggin Hill aerodrome, perhaps the most famous Battle of Britain air base. The battle was fought in the skies under which the 410 plied its trade, and schedules were often interrupted. A low railway bridge at Oxted meant that specially designed double-deckers were employed, and here we see one of the lowbridge STLs with a more or less standard provincial Weymann body pausing at the village green in Godstone, Surrey, on its way from Reigate to Bromley in about 1947. *Author's collection*

NEAR WESTERHAM: Successor of the lowbridge STL was another AEC Regent with a Weymann provincial-style body, and here No RLH17 (KYY 517), a design dating from 1950, begins the climb up the North Downs from above Westerham towards Biggin Hill on 29 December 1960.

Above: NEAR WESTERHAM: Green Line No RF125, en route from Sevenoaks to Windsor, can't quite hold off the Aston Martin as they ascend the North Downs beyond Westerham. The date is December 1977 when, officially, RFs had long been demoted from Green Line duties and only six were still at work with London Country, but no one seems to have told this Windsor-based vehicle. It was withdrawn the following month.

Left: OXTED: Eventually, by diverting the route away from a low bridge, normal-height buses could take over the 410, and here No RML2419 (JJD 419D) is seen in Bluehouse Lane, Oxted, Surrey, on a short working in 1977.

NEAR OXTED: London Country was losing customers and money fast throughout the 1970s, and went over to one-person operation as soon as possible. Eleven Daimler Fleetlines with Northern Counties bodies were delivered to Godstone garage in 1972 and took over the 410 route. Here No AF4 (JPK 104K) heads west along the A25 away from Old Oxted.

WESTERHAM is a delightful village beneath the North Downs, complete with village green and a statue of General Wolfe, the local hero who died conquering Quebec. It is seen here in 1926 with an East Surrey PS on route 403, travelling from Tonbridge to West Croydon and Wallington. Horse traffic was still commonplace then.

RTs arrived on the 403 from Chelsham and Dunton Green garages in the early months of 1950. Here preserved No RT3148 (KYY 877) recreates a Westerham scene of the early 1950s in the summer of 2014. *Author's collection*

WESTERHAM: Nos RF69 (DPD 537J) and SM537 (LYF 420) meet in Westerham in March 1976. The SMs, AEC Merins, had been ordered by London Transport but entered service with London Country, which was created in January 1970. They proved very unsatisfactory, adding to the company's woes.

WESTERHAM: Red buses now reach Westerham; on a sunny February afternoon in 2016 GoAhead MAN/MCV Enviro No 723 (AE09 DHV) sets off for Bromley. Behind is a G-Coach Enviro 200 laying over before returning to Sevenoaks.

WESTERHAM: Southdown Enviro 200 GX57 BXG, having made the descent from the North Downs, is about to make a right-hand turn in the middle of Westerham and head for Oxted, Godstone and Redhill on 7 February 2016.

CHARTWELL: The Leyland National was also used for a time as a Green Line coach, for which it was unsuited. No SNC138 (XPG 238N) of 1974 is seen here, when nearly new, in the coach park at Chartwell, Winston Churchill's home, at a time when the 706 route was extended here, a mile or so from Westerham, during the summer months. In the background is an elderly Bristol/ECW L-type bus.

DUNTON GREEN garage, near Sevenoaks, is seen on 3 April 1961. From left to right, the buses are No GS23 (MXX 323), one of the little one-man ECW-bodied Guys, three RTs Nos 2504 (KXW 133), 3669 (MXX 184) and 971 (JXC 499), and another GS.

The garage closed on 14 February 1998, and a row of houses stands on the site. However, we're sure you would prefer to see the beautifully cared-for bus shelter served by the 402 on the main road through Dunton Green today!

DUNTON GREEN: This close-up shows RTs Nos 79 (FXT 254) and 1039 (JXN 121) on 30 April 1961. The former was one of the 'pre-war' variety of RT, none of which originally worked in the Country Area, but in 1955 seven were repainted green to work from Hertford garage over a bridge with weight restrictions. Eventually they became trainers and, by a nice coincidence, green No RT79 took up residence for a while at Dunton Green.

A modified EFE model of No RT79 as a trainer at Dunton Green.

DUNTON GREEN: London Country's woes are epitomised by its having to resort to borrowing a wildly unsuitable Royal Blue ECW-bodied Bristol MW coach to work as a bus from Dunton Green. In this picture, dating from April 1976, it is accompanied by another ECW/Bristol vehicle, a London Country LH.

SEVENOAKS bus station was always most interesting, with its mix of London Transport and Maidstone & District buses. Here in about 1947 London Transport No STL237 (AGX 576) is working the 402 alongside a Maidstone & District TD4 bound for Maidstone; just glimpsed between them is a Maidstone & District coach. *Author's collection*

SEVENOAKS: Typical is this circa 1952 scene featuring an LT10T10 of 1938, which includes on its destination screen the intriguing name of 'Bat & Ball'. On the left an M&D conductor stands at the entrance of his 1947-vintage AEC Regal, while in the right background is an RT. *Author's collection*

SEVENOAKS: Maidstone & District continued to order lowbridge buses in the early post-war years, and here in Sevenoaks is a 1949-vintage Bristol K6A with a 53-seat Weymann body.

SEAL: FKL 609, a 1938 Maidstone & District Bristol K5G with a 1936 Weymann lowbridge body, heads through Seal on route 9 travelling from Sevenoaks to Maidstone in 1954.

SEVENOAKS: Moving on 23 years we see another bus on route 9, this time in Sevenoaks bus station, in July 1977. It is M&D Northern Counties-bodied Daimler Fleetline No 6084 (84 YKT) of 1964, alongside RPH 104L, a London Country ECW-bodied Bristol LH of 1973.

Sevenoaks's present-day bus station is a little further up the road in the town centre, and every summer a rally is held there where the once-familiar mix of London Transport and Maidstone & District vehicles springs, as if by magic, back to life. No RT604 (HLX 421) was the very last passenger-carrying RT in London Country service, nominally dating from 1948, and retaining National livery, which, although often and justifiably reviled, looked pretty good when pristine on an RT. It is standing alongside a Maidstone & District dual-purpose Willowbrook-bodied Leyland Leopard of 1968, OKO 816G.

SEVENOAKS: HKL 819 is a 1946 AEC Regal, converted to open top and is seen here reflected in a Sevenoaks shop windows as it speeds through the town with a full complement of jolly excursionists, including your author, on a sunny summer day in 2014.

LIMPSFIELD: Demonstrating just how rural the Country Area of London Transport could be, preserved RF MLL 533 heads up Limpsfield High Street, Surrey, on its way to Edenbridge in 2014.

EDENBRIDGE: A London Transport 1938-vintage 10T10 coach, demoted to bus duties, stands at Edenbridge in about 1948. *Author's collection*

EDENBRIDGE: In this 1977 scene London Country Leyland National No SNB206 (LPB 206P) sits ahead of Maidstone & District No 3273 (SKO 273P), a Plaxton-bodied Ford – a somewhat rare combination.

Today houses occupy the site of the garage, but opposite is this unidentified double-decker converted into a publicity vehicle for a bank, photographed in November 2015.

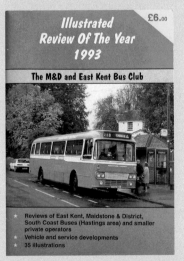

EDENBRIDGE: A somewhat surprising purchase by Maidstone & District in 1993 was six Alexander Y-bodied Leyland Leopards of 1978, which were sent to Edenbridge garage. No 3001 (TSJ 64S) is seen here working a local service in the town shortly after arriving from Scotland.

EDENBRIDGE: This April 2016 picture demonstrates just how attractive is Edenbridge's main street as Southdown UK55 ADZ approaches the main stopping place outside the Post Office on its way from East Grinstead, in Sussex, through Kent and over the River Eden, a tributary of the Medway, to its destination of Oxted, in Surrey.

NEAR HARTFIELD:
Metrobus No 6485 (YN53 RYX), a Scania/East Lancs Omnidekka, is caught near Hartfield, Sussex, in 2014 on its way west from Tunbridge Wells.

EAST GRINSTEAD:
Preserved former Maidstone & District Leyland Lynx No 3043 (E887 KYW) of 1988 is bound for Hartfield on the Tunbridge Wells road at East Grinstead in 2014.

FOREST ROW:
Metrobus No 627 (YN08 DFO), a Scania Omnicity of 2008, passes through Forest Row, East Sussex, on its way from East Grinstead to Tunbridge Wells in 2012.

Tonbridge and Tunbridge Wells

TONBRIDGE: Maidstone & District Dennis Falcon LKP 45 waits its next turn of duty beside Tonbridge station in 1955. There were just four of these little 20-seaters, dating from 1950, and they spent virtually all their careers in the Tonbridge area.

TONBRIDGE: Twelve all-Leyland lowbridge PD2 Titans were delivered to Maidstone & District in 1950. No DL25 (NKT 918) is seen at Tonbridge, also in 1955 ,working a relief on a route that did not need lowbridge buses.

TONBRIDGE: No 1001 (C201 EKJ), the first of the 20-seat Mercedes buses delivered in 1986, leaves Tonbridge station.

TONBRIDGE: Arriva No 4214 (KX61 FHM), an Optare Versa, heads across the River Medway in the town centre on its way from Tunbridge Wells to Bromley on 6 March 2016.

Top: TUNBRIDGE WELLS may have drawn visitors over the years on account of its spa status, but it has also been a fascinating place for bus enthusiasts. Timpsons was a very well-known London coach operator in post-war years, but it had also operated a bus network in Hastings, which was bought out by Maidstone & District in 1934. DY 7858 is a Harrington-bodied AEC Regent, dating only from a few months before the take-over; it became M&D No 107, fitted nicely into its fleet, and was transferred to Tunbridge Wells. Harrington built very few double-deck bodies and, although its coach bodies were much prized, particularly by M&D and Southdown, the company's bus bodies did not last well. No 107 had its body replaced in 1942, and its chassis did not last much longer, being broken up in 1948. *Author's collection*

Middle: TUNBRIDGE WELLS: Perhaps the best known of all routes serving Tunbridge Wells was the 122, a joint Southdown and M&D operation connecting the Sussex coast at Brighton with the Thames at Gravesend. In the first of these two June 1954 pictures we see a Southdown all-Leyland PD1 of 1947 on the route.

Bottom: TUNBRIDGE WELLS: This is also an all-Leyland bus, this time one of Maidstone & District's long-lived Farington PD2s with platform doors, delivered in 1951.

47

TUNBRIDGE WELLS: The replacement Weymann bodies fitted to the ex-Timpsons Regents in 1942 ended their days on later Regent chassis, namely six Regent IIIs. These were also based at Tunbridge Wells and one of them, No DH248 (JKM 105), is seen working a local service in October 1955. It is overtaking a Vauxhall Wyvern; no doubting the fact that Vauxhall was owned by General Motors of Detroit. Years later my brother-in-law briefly owned one, his pride and joy, but one of the hazards for the front-seat passenger, before the days of seat belts, was that on sharp corners one could slide across the bench seat and become entangled with the driver and steering wheel.

TUNBRIDGE WELLS: Photographed across the road in April 1955 is No DH355, another Weymann-bodied bus but this time a 1939-vintage Leyland TD5 Titan. A most handsome vehicle, it had recently been overhauled, despite a number of TD5s of this vintage having already been withdrawn. Indeed, this bus is listed as having been taken out of service in 1954, but there is no doubt that it was still at work four months into the following year.

TUNBRIDGE WELLS: Working route 7 at the town's West station terminus in June 1954 is No DH137 (HKE 238), a Bristol K6A of 1945 that had been fitted with a Weymann Orion body in February 1954. The Orion body generally was not a thing of beauty, but in the splendid lined dark green and pale cream M&D livery it could look quite appealing. This bus certainly earned its keep, not being withdrawn until 1967.

TUNBRIDGE WELLS: In this 1990 picture the handsome façade of Tunbridge Wells West station provides the backdrop to Green Line Leyland Tiger B273 KPF, its one-time through route to Windsor now extending no further than Bromley.

Tunbridge Wells West is now no longer a railway station, but the prominent clock tower survives, seen here in 2011 beyond the parked Countryliner Dennis Dart KM51 BFN.

TUNBRIDGE WELLS:
Normally the only London
Transport vehicles to reach the
town were Green Line coaches,
but during the Second World
War an emergency service was
operated with double-deck
buses, and here No STL1147
(CGJ 141) is about to set off for
Victoria. Note the boarded-up
windows, damaged by bomb
blast. *Author's collection*

TUNBRIDGE WELLS:
One of the long-lived Leyland
Leopards (EKJ 447K) climbs
Grosvenor Road in 1992.

TUNBRIDGE WELLS: Also on Grosvenor Road, which becomes Mount Pleasant Road, is an almost new Plaxton-bodied Dennis Dart dating from 1992, outside one of the town's grandest buildings.

TUNBRIDGE WELLS: This handsome vehicle, No SO68 (RKE 540), was a joint Saunders Roe and Maidstone & District project, and was the latter company's very first underfloor-engine single-decker. It entered service in 1953 and served a creditable 13 years for a one-off before being sold in 1966. It is seen here in October 1955 setting off on a journey much of which will be along the River Medway and Eden valleys, terminating in Edenbridge.

TUNBRIDGE WELLS: Inside the town's garage in 1955 is a Leyland TD1 of 1928, converted into a towing truck, which lasted until 1959, and a 1949 Harrington-bodied AEC Mark III Regal. The lady could be either 'Gert' or 'Daisy', wartime radio characters played by Elsie and Doris Waters (sisters of actor Jack Warner). Don't know what I'm talking about? Never mind…

Inside the garage in 1998 are two Kentish Bus Olympians, a former Ribble Burlingham-bodied PD2 repainted in traditional Maidstone & District livery, and No 3617, a Plaxton-bodied Volvo.

TUNBRIDGE WELLS: Over the years the 402 route, already encountered in the previous chapter, has led a most interesting life. For a time, like its companion the 403, it became a red bus route, as illustrated here in 1998 by a pair of Plaxton-bodied Dart Pointers, operated by Arriva Kent & Sussex.

TUNBRIDGE WELLS: No SO713 (FKO 55), an Eastern Coachworks-bodied Leyland TS8 Tiger of 1939, stands outside the garage in November 1954.

Left: **TUNBRIDGE WELLS:** 1986 saw an influx into the area of Mercedes minibuses bodied by Rootes (a local firm), of which No 1009 (C209 EKJ) is an example.

Below: **TUNBRIDGE WELLS:** A long-lived Maidstone & District all-Leyland PD2, NKT 906, braves snow flurries by Tunbridge Wells Common in January 1969.

TUNBRIDGE WELLS: Arriva Southern Counties Wright Bus Streetlite No 4278 (GN64 DXW) swings around by Tunbridge Wells Common in November 2015.

TUNBRIDGE WELLS: Brighton & Hove now operates the Brighton to Tunbridge Wells route 29. This go-ahead company names all its buses, and this one, passing Tunbridge Wells Common also in November 2015, commemorates Wynne Baxter, a well-known solicitor and the first Mayor of Lewes.

Dartford and Gravesend

DARTFORD: A Bexley & Dartford Joint Committee former LCC B-type four-wheel tram heads down the hill to the town centre in 1927. Dartford's original fleet of trams was completely destroyed in a depot fire in 1917. *Author's collection*

DARTFORD: Three D2-type trolleybuses of 1936 wait in the town centre in about 1958, with an AEC Mercury tower wagon in the distance and an RT just visible on the right. *Author's collection*

Above: DARTFORD: In about 1950 London Transport No STL1363 (CLX 586) is working one of the Country Area's shortest routes, extending not much more than a mile from Littlebrook power station to the town centre and football ground. *Author's collection*

Right: DARTFORD: No RMC1480 (480 CLT), a double-deck Routemaster coach downgraded to bus work from Dartford garage, takes part in the Historic Commercial Vehicle Club (HCVC) run to Brighton in 1977.

DARTFORD: Kentish Bus Leyland Lynx G41 VME stands in Dartford town centre in the summer of 1996.

DARTFORD: Much of the town centre has been transformed over the decades since the 1950s. In 2006 Selkent Alexander-bodied Dennis Trident No 17163 (V163 MEV) of 1999 is working the trolleybus replacement route 96, which terminates at the vast Bluewater retail outlet.

Left: **DARTFORD:** Stagecoach Enviro 400 No 19810 (LX11 BJZ) is seen on the 96 at the same location ten years later on 4 April 2016.

Below: **DARTFORD:** Dartford Fastrack Wright-bodied Volvo GN06 EWE, heading for Gravesend, passes a Plaxton-bodied Dennis Dart on route 428.

GRAVESEND is perhaps the most attractive of the Thames-side towns, certainly down by the historic waterfront, where the pilots of the Port of London Authority have their headquarters. Parked just off the town centre is Maidstone & District No SO15 (HKL 825), a Beadle-bodied AEC Regal of 1946.

GRAVESEND: London Transport one-man-operated 20-seat Leyland Cub No C73 (BXD 698) of 1935 is seen in the town centre in about 1949.

Almost 70 years later, on 4 April 2016, Arriva Dennis Sapphire Enviro 400 GN58 BSX awaits passengers in the town centre.
Author's collection/author

GRAVESEND: Arriva Streetlite GN64 DXG speeds along West Street on 4 April 2016.

Maidstone

WEST MALLING: I had the great good luck (ha-ha) to serve Her Majesty as a Senior Aircraftsman typist at RAF West Malling, a few miles west of Maidstone, in 1957, and here I am after my very first flight. It had been in an Anson, which flew down to the Kent coast, right around Ramsgate, Broadstairs and Margate, up the Thames Estuary – over which I got sick – then back to base. Beyond the Anson you can just make out the Meteor night-fighters, of which there were three squadrons.

WEST MALLING: A rebodied former Maidstone & District Leyland Tiger coach dating from 1931, by then in the possession of Kent County Constabulary, stands outside the guardroom at RAF West Malling in the summer of 1957.

WEST MALLING: All sorts of things happen today on the site of RAF West Malling, including Arriva Alexander-bodied Volvo No 6449, GN04 UFV, which is passing roughly over the spot where my friend, Joe Hyam from Golders Green, served as education clerk. Joe had a BA from Oxford but for reasons I never quite fathomed refused to take an RAF trade test and proudly displayed on his door 'Education Clerk, J. Hyam, BA, Aircraftsman Second Class'.

WEST MALLING: Maidstone & District Saunders-bodied Bristol K6A No DH230 of 1948 waits for the traffic to clear so it can leave West Malling and continue on its way to Maidstone in 1957.

Left: WEST MALLING: Grey Green No 807 (SPC 265R), a former London Country Leyland National, was photographed at West Malling in October 1994.

Below: WEST MALLING: On the opposite side of the elegant High Street in April 2016 is an equally rather elegant Arriva Wright-bodied Volvo hybrid.

Above: **DETLING: Across the Medway valley east of Maidstone was the satellite RAF Detling, which by 1957 was seeing limited use by the RAF. Now it is a showground, and during the South East Bus Rally there in April 2016 we were able to see part of this wonderful collection of East Kent vehicles, that being the company's centenary celebration year.**

Left: **DETLING: Preserved No DL39 (VKR 39) was giving rides. It is a Park Royal-bodied Mark V AEC Regent and an example of the very last Maidstone & District half cabs, dating from 1956.**

DETLING: A nice contrast on that day was Arriva Wright-bodied Volvo No 7010 (KX13 AVR) and one of the all-time classics, No DH379 (NKT 875), an all-Leyland PD2 of 1951. Visible in the background are a Maidstone Corporation Leyland Titan and an East Kent Regent.

MAIDSTONE: Before the days of motorways, the A20, passing through Maidstone, was one of the two principal routes from London to Dover. In this scene, which must date from only just after the First World War – note the parked tank (no, sorry, I don't know what it was doing there) – two open charabancs are among an eclectic collection of vehicles heading eastward over the River Medway.

In the second view Maidstone & District No 5722 (LJA 626P) sets off over the Medway Bridge for West Malling in December 1994.

Finally, more than two decades later Arriva East Lancashire-bodied Dennis Trident No 5442 (T405 SMV) is seen at the same location in April 2016. *KPA Goulding/ author (2)*

MAIDSTONE: Two East Kent routes reached Maidstone. The celebrated route 10 extended to within sight of France at Folkestone, and here in 1954 an East Kent TD4, with a post-war Park Royal body, prepares for its journey to the shores of the English Channel.

MAIDSTONE: The other joint route into Maidstone was the 67. GFN 916 is a 1953-vintage Guy Arab with a Park Royal body, which clearly owes a great deal to the RT bodies that Park Royal was producing at that time.

MAIDSTONE: In this mid-1930s scene a Ransomes trolleybus, KO 8892, in seen in the town centre, with another in the background. One cannot help but comment that, while early trolleybuses looked pretty up-to-date from the rear, from the front they looked positively primitive. *KPA Goulding*

MAIDSTONE: Corporation trolleybus No 88 (BDY 817), formerly a Hastings vehicle, leads 1959 Massey-bodied Leyland PD2 Titan No 14 (414 GKT) in Knightrider Street.

MAIDSTONE: In the High Street at the end of the 1930s a Maidstone & District Titan bus can be seen in the distance heading away from the camera.

In the second picture we see Boro'line No 240 (CKM 140Y), also in the High Street. Towards the end if its existence the company made some very questionable acquisitions, among them this Bedford, a make that was once enormously popular but was about to disappear.

In October 1994 East Kent Leyland National No 1181 (NFR 81R) of 1977 (the year East Kent adopted fleet numbers) sets off up the High Street on route 10 to Ashford. *Author's collection (2)/author*

MAIDSTONE: Said to have been the first bus station in the country when it opened in Palace Avenue, Maidstone, in 1922, a collection of mostly very early Leyland Tigers and some Tilling-Stevens are on display in about 1932. *Author's collection*

MAIDSTONE: At the bus station in November 1954, flanking No DH227 (JKM 924), a Saunders-bodied Bristol K6A of 1947, are two Daimler CWA6s of 1943, their wartime bodies replaced by Weymann ones in 1951.

MAIDSTONE: With the collapse of Boro'line in 1992 Maidstone & District moved into its Armstrong Road depot, and inside it we see a Northern Counties Olympian and a Maidstone & District coach; the latter is carrying the Green Line fleet name, the Maidstone to London service having become part of the Green Line network at that time.

MAIDSTONE: The Tilling-Stevens factory was in Maidstone and, until overtaken by Leyland and AEC at the beginning of the 1930s, the company was one of the country's leading suppliers of buses and coaches. A remarkable survivor is this Maidstone & District 1928 B9A with a Short Brothers body.

MAIDSTONE: Crossley will always be a make associated with its home city of Manchester but, although rare in the South of England, Crossleys did manage to sell vehicles to Portsmouth and Maidstone corporations. On first seeing a 1938 Maidstone Mancunian, such as the one pictured here, I was struck by how remarkably old-fashioned it looked compared with other contemporary Maidstone & District buses. *Author's collection*

MAIDSTONE: Former Chatham & District Bristol K5G GKR 749 of 1942, rebodied by Weymann in 1951 and taken into the Maidstone & District fleet as No DH441, is seen at Maidstone in 1958 preparing to head for Chatham. It was withdrawn in 1960.

CHELSHAM: In order to help London Country keep its show on the road in the late 1970s, Maidstone Borough Council lent the company a number of its Massey-bodied Atlanteans. One is seen here at Chelsham garage, near Warlingham, Surrey, in 1977, between No RT1018, a Leyland National, and No RMC1511.

Left: MAIDSTONE: A real sign of desperate times was this East Lancs-bodied Leyland Atlantean of 1974, acquired in 1990 and not even repainted into its new owner's livery.

Below: MAIDSTONE: Leyland Lynx F45 ENF, a 1991-vintage bus taken over from Shearings, is on 'Park & Ride' duties in the town in December 1994.

The Medway towns

GILLINGHAM: A Harrington-bodied AEC Reliance coach is being prepared in a yard in Gillingham in September 1967 for a journey with a group calling themselves the Overlanders, which will take it through Europe and on across Turkey, Iran, Afghanistan, Pakistan and India to Nepal, organised by Janet Hammond, a nurse from Gravesend. The coach had originated with Grey-Green, a long-established coach firm that ran between London and various resorts, including the Kent ones, and would eventually become Arriva. Maidstone & District owned a fleet of almost identical vehicles.

KABUL: A previous Overlanders trip in a Yeates-bodied Maudslay set out from Gillingham in March 1966, and is seen on arrival in the Afghanistan capital, Kabul, three months later.

GILLINGHAM: An all-Leyland Maidstone & District PD2 (NKT 892) heads home for its depot at Luton, Chatham, in September 1968.

GILLINGHAM: A former London bus (PJ53 SRO) sets out from Luton depot early on the morning of 2 April 2016 on railway replacement duties.

Above: BRIGHTON: Quite the oldest former Maidstone & District vehicle is this wonderful Halford of 1908, once used between Gravesend and Chatham, and seen here on completing the Historic Commercial Vehicle Club run to Brighton in May 2015.

Right: CHATHAM A splendid collection of Chatham & District buses in Chatham town centre in about 1946.

CHATHAM: In the historic dockyard, Royal Navy sloop HMS *Gannet* of 1878 can be seen behind preserved 1972 Maidstone & District Leyland Leopard EKJ 448K.

Below left: **DETLING: Just one former Chatham & District bus survives. This is GKE 68, a Weymann-bodied Bristol K5G of 1939. Although seen here only in skeletal form at the South Eastern Bus Show at Detling in April 2016, much sound work has been done towards its complete restoration.**

Below: **A rather nice Corgi model of a wartime Chatham & District Bristol.**

DORSET: A former, much modified – or, rather, hacked about – Chatham & District Leyland TD1 of 1930 survived, just about, until the early 1980s in this scrapyard near Blandford Forum in Dorset. Your author was given permission to photograph it by the yard owner, who, as an afterthought, remarked, 'Mind the dog.' Unfortunately the dog minded the author, taking a firm grip with its teeth on his left hand, although without leaving any marks, until persuaded to let go.

CHATHAM: Maidstone & District invested in a number of ex-London Transport DMS Daimlers and found them rather more to their liking than had their original owners. This one is working a Chatham local service in February 1989.

CHATHAM: At the Pentagon bus station on 27 March 1993 are two Maidstone & District Dennis double-deckers, and a Mercedes approaching. The Pentagon shopping centre, complete with bus station, was opened in 1976. Chatham could have done with an attractive piece of modern architecture in the town centre to complement the rather jolly town hall, but the Pentagon was definitely not it. The gloomy, fume-ridden bus station was a good example of all that was wrong with the treatment of bus passengers at that time. The second view shows the closed Pentagon bus station on 2 April 2016.

Meanwhile, the Waterfront bus station was opened opposite the Pentagon. While of much more pleasing aspect, there have been justifiable complaints of its propensity to funnel wind where it is not needed. In the third picture, taken at dawn on 2 April 2016, a lone passenger will no doubt welcome the warm interior of the Sapphire Enviro 400 working route 101 to Maidstone.

CHATHAM: A Leyland Lynx descends Bluebell Hill, Chatham, on its way to Maidstone in 1994, then on 2 April 2016 a Nu-Venture Dart is at the same location heading for Chatham.

ROCHESTER: Trams of the Chatham & District Light Railways Company, founded in 1902, ran along 3ft 6in-gauge tracks in Rochester High Street, as can be seen in this contemporary postcard. The trams were replaced by buses in 1930, but the light green and light brown livery was retained.

ROCHESTER's High Street, with its ancient buildings, Dickensian associations, cathedral and castle, probably brings more visitors to the Medway towns than even the historic Chatham Dockyard. With its crowds of pedestrians, seen here in April 2016, it seems inconceivable the narrow High Street was once part of one of Britain's most important routes, the Roman road that later became the A2, linking London with Dover and hence to the continent.

ROCHESTER: A bypass was eventually built for the A2, and this picture dates from the end of the 1990s when the attractive post-NBC livery, designed by Ray Stenning with echoes of the traditional Maidstone & District one, was being superseded by that of Arriva. Both buses are Northern Counties-bodied Olympians; route 133 connected Cliffe with the Medway towns.

ROCHESTER: A former London Transport Routemaster, converted to open-top format, heads west along the A2 in 2000.

ASHFORD: The town's East Kent garage is seen in 1954 with a collection of ECW and Park Royal Leyland Titan TD4s and 5s together with two pre-war Dennis Lancets, the furthest dating from 1936 with the older, less elegant-looking radiator.

ASHFORD: Outside the garage in 1954 is 1937 Dennis Lancet JG 8708 with a 1948 Park Royal body.

ASHFORD: Both East Kent and Maidstone & District had garages in Station Road, which were joined. In 1960 outside the latter's facility is East Kent Park Royal-bodied Dennis Lancet CFN 131 of 1948, with a modernised front end. *Author's collection*

ASHFORD: This is the East Kent garage in 1974 with a Bristol/ECW VR inside. A new garage on the Brunswick Road industrial estate replaced the former adjacent garages in 1976.

ASHFORD: An East Kent Stagecoach Solo passes the site of the old garage in Station Road in January 2016.

ASHFORD: A Stagecoach Alexander-bodied Dennis Trident arrives at Ashford bus station working route 10 in 2009.

Above: TENTERDEN: In 1990 Maidstone & District Bristol VR BKE 857T is adorned with a special 75th anniversary livery depicting historic buses.

Above: TENTERDEN: An East London coach arrives on a day trip to the Kent & East Sussex Railway in December 1994.

TENTERDEN: 1987-vintage Arriva Lynx E890 KYW stands beside Transweald Dart No 3210 (P210 LKJ) in about 2000.

LYDD: A Stagecoach Alexander-bodied Scania splashes across the marshes as it approaches Lydd on a January afternoon in 2016.

LYDD: Photographed in January 2016, this skilfully converted residence was once an East Kent dormitory garage.

Above: **DUNGENESS: An outpost of the East Kent empire was Dungeness nuclear power station.** Here a preserved Park Royal-bodied AEC Regent of 1959 passes the power station on 4 September 2016.

Left and below: **HYTHE: Despite being resolutely confounded on each visit, I return again and again to Dover and Folkestone, each time hoping that the proximity of these twin ports to France will finally be evidenced by – well, by what? The inhabitants donning striped shirts and berets and dancing the can-can in the streets, or driving about in Deux Chevauxs and Traction Avants? Might East Kent purchase a fleet of open-rear-platform, high-sided retro-style TN4Cs, while their crews regularly strike for shorter hours and higher pensions? But it never happens, and today, despite some of the buses and coaches being labelled to serve cross-Channel ferries, in all other respects they are resolutely British. We begin with CGJ 987, East Kent's one and only all-Leyland PD2, seen on a damp lunchtime at Hythe early in January 1960, the last exposure I had left after my first visit to Paris.**

Fifty-six years later Stagecoach Transbus Dart No 34482 (SV53 DDJ) speeds past the Military Canal at the same location on a school run in January 2016.

SANDGATE is an attractive location right on the edge of the English Channel, immediately to the west of and adjoining Folkestone. In Edwardian times this horse-drawn tramway connected it with that town.

In the same setting the best part of 100 years later, a Stagecoach East Kent Alexander-bodied Scania passes, bound for Hythe. Forming the background are Folkestone and the Leas, where can be found some of the finest of all English late-Victorian and Edwardian seaside architecture.

SANDGATE: A Stagecoach East Kent Trident heads into the sunset in 2011, while another Stagecoach East Kent Scania is on its way westwards towards Folkestone in January 2016. Despite claiming to be not in service, it seems to be doing good business as it overtakes an early-morning jogger.

FOLKESTONE: In this rare pre-war colour picture at Folkestone, a Tilling-Stevens bus is sandwiched between two East Kent TS7/8 Tiger Park Royal-bodied coaches, while a Southern Railway (former SECR) 4-4-0 crosses the great viaduct spanning the town.

In January 2016 Stagecoach East Kent Dennis Dart No 34483 (SV53 DDK) dives down from Folkestone town centre on a local service. *Colour Rail/author*

FOLKESTONE: East Kent Park Royal-bodied Guy Arab EFN 179 of 1950 is captured in the town centre in about 1950. In the same location today buses no longer come this way. *Author's collection/ author*

FOLKESTONE: Seen here is one of 30 Marshall-bodied Leyland Leopards that East Kent bought from Southdown in 1971 when one-man operation was being planned for the town. *Author's collection*

FOLKESTONE: East Kent bought a number of Leyland Titans from London Transport. In this 1998 picture the low February sun lights up No 7209 (OHV 769Y) with the cliffs between Folkestone and Dover forming the background.

FOLKESTONE: Over the years East Kent has had many connections with the port, and here in the late 1980s a 1975-vintage Leyland National in Seacat livery is seen in the town's bus station together with a Leyland Olympian and an Iveco minibus.

FOLKESTONE: At the bus station in 1987 are East Kent Metrobus No 7761 (F761 EKM) on route 10, and ECW-bodied VR Bristol XJJ 657V bound for Lydd on route 11.

FOLKESTONE: Two East Kent Metrobuses stand in the bus station in June 1992.

FOLKESTONE: While not exactly outstanding, the several-times-rebuilt Folkestone bus station is not without architectural merit and, unlike some, certainly does its best to create a welcoming environment. This photograph dates from August 2015.

FOLKESTONE: A dawn scene in January 2016 sees Stagecoach East Kent Enviro 400 No 15188 (YN64 AKX) getting ready to depart from Folkestone for Canterbury.

FOLKESTONE: Night time at the bus station in February 2016, with Solo No 47685 (GN58 PXM).

FOLKESTONE: For a number of years while the Channel Tunnel was being constructed, and for some time afterwards, there was a fascinating exhibition centre overlooking the site and explaining all about the amazing technology that was allowing this age-old dream to come to fruition. A just-delivered 1991-vintage East Kent 85-seat Olympian, H801 BKK, is parked outside waiting for a tour party.

Now long closed as an exhibition centre, the site is still in existence, as seen in the second picture, from January 2016.

In the third view a local Folkestone service passes a few hundred yards from the site. Stagecoach Solo No 47114 (GX54 DXM) is ready to return to Folkestone town centre in January 2016.

DOVER: The night after a Second World War raid on the town, a Park Royal-bodied Leyland TD5 Titan stands on the edge of chaos. This is a company publicity photograph, the bus having been driven around the town and parked in a number of damaged locations. *M&D and East Kent Bus Club*

DOVER: In the garage in the early 1960s are, from left to right, a Southdown Beadle-bodied Leyland Tiger Cub, three East Kent Guy Arabs, and one all-Leyland PD1. *Author's collection*

THE CAR FERRY, DOVER HARBOUR

DOVER: The first view shows the now barely recognisable Western Docks in Sealink days, some time in the early 1960s. Just one unidentifiable coach is visible, parked outside the terminal building. Half a century later, on 23 August 2016, a coach boards a ferry, with a P&O vessel in the background. *Author's collection/author*

DOVER: This line-up in about 1985 comprises a 1967-vintage Park Royal-bodied AEC Regent, a former Southdown Daimler Fleetline in P&O livery, and an ECW-bodied Leyland Leopard coach of 1982. *Author's collection*

Left: DOVER: Seen here are two Park Royal-bodied AEC Regents of 1967, the one on the left in East Kent livery, that on the right in the far more sombre and less attractive National Bus Company red. *Author's collection*

Below: DOVER: This is a former London Transport AEC Merlin of 1970 belonging to Townsend Thoresen in about 1980.

DOVER: Leaving the familiar Docks area is an Alexander-bodied AEC Swift of 1971. Behind is a Plaxton-bodied coach in National Express livery. *Author's collection*

Left: **DOVER:** The cross-Channel ferry *Pride of Canterbury* leaves Dover for Calais in 2015, with the one of the company's Optare port buses in the foreground.

Below: **DOVER:** A National Express coach begins the spectacular climb out of Dover over the Western Docks in January 2016.

The Promenade and Pier, Deal.

DEAL is seen in 1920 with two East Kent 1919-vintage AEC/Daimlers with Hora bodies. These buses regularly worked to Canterbury, but lasted only two years with the company.

In January 2016 a Stagecoach East Kent Enviro 200 heads west at the same location.

SANDWICH: Park Royal-bodied East Kent AEC Regent WFN 831 is seen in this picturesque town after delivery on 28 May 1970.

In Sandwich in August 1998 are East Kent single-deckers Nos 661 and 641 (K791 DAO and (N641 LPN). *M&D and East Kent Bus Club/author*

SANDWICH: The town's East Kent ticket office is now preserved.

SANDWICH: Stagecoach Olympian No 7803 (H803 BKK) crosses the Sandwich-Minster railway line in August 1998, with the White Mill of 1760 in the background.

Canterbury and North Kent

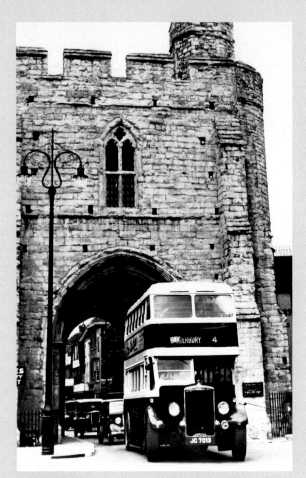

Left: **CANTERBURY: Throughout the year** visitors from all over the world throng the city and pilgrims have been coming since the cathedral was established in AD 597, especially since the martyrdom of Thomas à Becket in 1170. The first railway in southern England was the Canterbury & Whitstable, and although that closed in 1952 Stagecoach East Kent covers the journey today in just 29 minutes. The first regular bus service to serve the city was around 1910, and in September 1916 the East Kent Road Car Company was born here. JG 7013, a Park Royal-bodied Leyland TD4 Titan of 1936 with original, limited route indicator, passes through the West Gate in about 1938. *Author's collection*

Below: **CANTERBURY: To mark the centenary** of the East Kent Road Car Company, Stagecoach did a fine job of turning out Alexander-bodied Scania No 15443 (KX08 KZK) in a wonderful retro livery. It is seen here passing the site of St Peter's bus station on 24 May 2016.

CANTERBURY: As in the wartime Dover picture, this scene has been posed by the East Kent company, showing children rushing into a shelter and featuring Titan AJG 5. *M&D and East Kent Bus Club*

CANTERBURY: East Kent inherited five Weymann-bodied Daimler COG5s from the operator of the Thanet trams, the Isle of Thanet Electric Supply Company, in 1937. One of them is seen here in Canterbury in use during the war as a mobile staff canteen. *M&D and East Kent Bus Club*

CANTERBURY: This is St Peter's bus station in about 1943. Prominent are two East Kent Park Royal-bodied Leyland TD4 Titans; that on the right, JG 7823, has its formerly cream-painted areas now in wartime grey. Beyond are two 1936 Dennis Lancets. I regret that I cannot identify the pram in the right foreground… *Author's collection*

CANTERBURY: A wartime Guy Arab working a local Canterbury service in about 1950. *Author's collection*

CANTERBURY: Two preserved 1956 Park Royal-bodied Guy Arabs, MFN 898 and MFN 888, pass Canterbury's city walls on 3 September 2016.

CANTERBURY: Plaxton-bodied Volvo No 3187 (WVT 618), new to Wallace Arnold in 1966, stands at the city's bus station in about 1980.

CANTERBURY: At the East Kent bus station in 1990 are, on the left, a briefly popular but short-lived Ford minibus of 1986, then a Metrobus of 1988 and, just sneaking into the picture, a Bristol/ECW VR.

Left: **CANTERBURY: Brand-new Stagecoach East Kent Alexander-bodied Scania No 15273 boards passengers at the bus station on 24 May 2016.**

Below: **CANTERBURY: No, as far as we know this isn't really a pirate, and neither is Stagecoach East Kent Alexander Dennis Enviro 20D No 36855 doing meal deals at the city's bus station on the same day!**

Left: **CANTERBURY:** Stagecoach bio Unibus GN13 HJK turns into Kent University, Turing Campus, with the cathedral dominating the city skyline, on 26 August 2016.

Below: **CANTERBURY:** Even in their excellent original East Kent livery, the Park Royal-bodied AEC Bridgemasters were not particularly good-looking, and the all-over training yellow applied by the National Bus Company revealed them to be some of the ugliest buses ever built. Two are seen outside the Canterbury works in about 1980. As can be seen, East Kent and Maidstone & District very nearly amalgamated.

CANTERBURY: Seen in 1980 is a most attractive vehicle, a 1970-vintage Plaxton-bodied AEC Reliance coach in traditional East Kent livery, now preserved.

RAMSGATE: Looking down on Ramsgate Harbour in the 1920s, one of the Isle of Thanet trams ascending.

In a similar view in the 1930s, shortly after the trams had disappeared, the bus making its steady way downwards looks like a Tilling-Stevens. *Both author's collection*

RAMSGATE: How to dress at the seaside in the early 1920s. This is The Paragon, Ramsgate, with the harbour beyond. Tram tracks are in place, but no tram is in evidence. *Author's collection*

RAMSGATE: At the harbour in 1950, London Transport No RT2063 (LYF 1), with another RT behind, down for a weekend trip to the seaside, is heading home. There is an East Kent Guy Arab behind them, while down beside the water is a fleet of East Kent Leyland Tiger coaches.

RAMSGATE might have been the preserve of East Kent, but Maidstone & District coaches were regular visitors. This all-Leyland Royal Tiger, No CO283 (OKO 31), was one of 14 that arrived in 1952 and was largely used on excursion work. It is seen here parked up by the sea in 1954.

RAMSGATE: An East Kent Leyland Titan PD1 and TD4 rub noses beside the Harbour in the summer of 1959.

RAMSGATE: East Kent AEC Regent 5/Park Royal MFN 944F does a smart turn away from the Harbour in about 1975.

Forty years later, in January 2016, it is a Stagecoach Alexander-bodied Volvo Olympian that is turning away from the Harbour. *Author's collection/author*

RAMSGATE:
In August 1998
Stagecoach Metrobus
F773 EKM is centre
stage at the Harbour.
In a similar view in
January 2016 three
Stagecoach East
Kent Enviro 20Ds
are working the Loop
connecting Ramsgate,
Broadstairs and
Margate.

MARGATE has long been popular with holidaymakers and day-trippers from London, arriving by boat, train and coach. In this postcard, bought by the author's grandparents in 1910, a tram of the Isle of Thanet Electric Tramways & Lighting Co, one of the four-wheel American-built cars dating from the system's opening in 1901, is doing good business, the only competition seemingly horse-drawn.

Below left and below:
MARGATE: Looking eastward in 1918, once again it is summer time, the sands are crowded, and two trams are going about their business. The trams connected Margate, Broadstairs and Ramsgate, much of the journey along the sea front. There were 40 cars in all; 20 had bogies, but these proved troublesome and were soon converted to four-wheelers. The system lasted until 1937, when East Kent buses took over.

Almost a century later, on 25 August 2016, the hottest day of the year (34°C), a Stagecoach East Kent Scania Alexander Dennis of 2016 passes several thousand holidaymakers.

113

MARGATE: For many years East Kent operated open-top buses along the Thanet coast, and this 1945 Park Royal-bodied Guy Arab was one of the first to be adapted for this task.

HERNE BAY: An East Kent Marshall-bodied AEC Swift is seen in Station Road in 1969. *M&D and East Kent Bus Club*

HERNE BAY: Often threatened with closure, Herne Bay garage was still open in April 2016, and carries a commemorative plaque describing its place in East Kent history.

EAST KENT
ROAD CAR COMPANY LTD

Was founded on
11th August 1916

by the amalgamation of
WACHER OF HERNE BAY,
who owned this site,
with four other
local bus companies

FAVERSHAM: Five fine Faversham-based Maidstone & District bus men pose in front of KE 1385, a Dodson-bodied Tilling-Stevens of 1920. *Author's collection*

FAVERSHAM was very much border territory, shared by East Kent and Maidstone & District. Here is an East Kent Park Royal-bodied Regent V of 1961. *M&D and East Kent Bus Club*

FAVERSHAM: Of late an absolute must for vintage bus and coach connoisseurs in Kent has been the annual transport festival in this attractive North Kent town. The preserved vehicles are parked all over the town, giving not just enthusiasts but also the general public an opportunity to get up close and intimate and, in a number cases, ride on the vehicles. Featured in the first of this series of pictures of the event are three former M&D double-deckers, on the left an Alexander-bodied Ailsa and Bristol/ECW VR, and on the right an Invictaway ECW-bodied Leyland Olympian.

FAVERSHAM: East Kent Park Royal-bodied Daimler Freeline RFN 953G of 1969.

117

FAVERSHAM: Buggies and buses.

FAVERSHAM: No S6 (BKT 821C), a Maidstone & District Marshall bodied AEC Reliance of 1965.

FAVERSHAM: 390 DKK started out with Maidstone & District in 1958 as a Harrington-bodied AEC Reliance coach, but in 1963 had a new front grafted on and became a bus.

FAVERSHAM: HKE 867, an M&D Bristol K6A of 1945 with a 1953 Weymann body, gives lucky patrons a ride around the town.

FAVERSHAM: Its nose poking out of the former M&D garage, now owned by South Eastern Coachworks, is newly restored Plaxton-bodied Bedford OB EAJ 679 of 1948.

FAVERSHAM: Finally, present-day Stagecoach East Kent Alexander-bodied Dennis Trident No 18163 (GX54 DVF) pulls out past East Kent Daimler Freeline/Park Royal RFN 953G of 1969.

Kentish miscellany

1930: East Kent was a very good customer of Tilling-Stevens, until it could not keep up with the advances made by Leyland and Dennis. JG 669, a Brush-bodied Tilling-Stevens B10 of 1930, has most fortunately been preserved and is a great favourite on the rally circuit. It is seen here at the Chalkpits Museum at Amberley in 2014. The second picture shows the interior.

1930/31: East Kent invested in a fleet of ten all-Leyland TD1s in 1930/31, a big leap forward on anything seen previously in the company's fleet. Several were loaned to other companies during the war, but four lasted with East Kent until 1948.

1937: JG 9938 is a preserved Park Royal-bodied Leyland TS7 Tiger of 1937. The advance in design, both inside and out, in the seven years between this and the previous pictures is extraordinary.

Admittedly the Tilling-Stevens is a bus and the Tiger a coach, but as we can see from the interior of a 1937 Dennis Lancet (third picture) bus design had also leapt ahead.

1930s: I wonder just who are the lucky gents surrounded by this bevy of lovely ladies and where are they off to in two late-1930s Maidstone & District coaches? One can only guess at the date, which may be just before the Second World War. *Author's collection*

1939-40: This line-up consists of ten East Kent wartime Austerity Guy Arabs. In all, the company was allocated 18 highbridge buses such as these, and 45 lowbridge vehicles. *M&D and East Kent Bus Club*

1950/2016: A Grey-Green Harrington-bodied Leyland Royal Tiger of 1950 is on its way to the Kent coast.

Since the early post-war years the number of passenger vehicles arriving from the continent, whether for day trips or longer, has grown out of all recognition, virtually all of them arriving by ferry at Dover or through the Channel Tunnel. Here a French coach hurries along the M2, London-bound, on 24 May 2016. *Author's collection/author*

1951: East Kent Park Royal-bodied Royal Tiger FFN 449 of 1951 stands at Battersea Park between trips to and from Lympne Airport.

Fortunately one of these highly distinctive vehicles has been preserved, by Ensign, a rare example of the very first generation of underfloor-engined coaches.

1954: HJG 25, a handsome but not entirely successful Duple Ambassador-bodied Dennis Lancet UF of 1954, gets ready to convey Paris-bound adventurers.

Below: **1959:** Parked on the left, former East Kent Park Royal-bodied AEC Regent V PFN 853 of 1959 is on London sightseeing duties in Tavistock Place in 1998.

Right: DORCHESTER: Van Hool-bodied Scania JK14 JNK of Jay & Kay of Crayford loads up outside Dorchester market in February 2016. A visit to this market is a favourite feature of any coach trip to the West Country for those in search of a bit of Thomas Hardy atmosphere.

Right: SWANAGE: An East Kent Scania/Berkhof is parked in the forecourt of Swanage station, deep in Wilts & Dorset territory, in July 1997.

Index of locations and operators